LEARN MALAYALAM IN AUSTRALIA WITH JESUS

Written & Illustrated by
Dr. Abraham Thomas Eettickal

VOWELS 1

അ

A

അനുഗ്രഹം

Anu- gra-ham

BLESSING- The Lord bless you and keep you.(Numbers 6:24)

ഇ

E

ഇടയൻ

E-da-yan

SHEPHERD- Jesus is the Shepherd of us all.

ഇ ഇ

ഇ ഇ

Ee

ഈയോബ്

Ee- yo-bu

JOB- is a rightous man who withstands the test of his faith in God (Read the Book of Job in the Bible)

ഈ ഈ

ഈ ഈ

U
ഉയർപ്പ്
U-yar-ppu

RESURRECTION- The resurrection of Christ from the dead, marks the dawn of Christinanity (Ephesians 1:20)

ഊ

Uu

ഊന്നുവടി
Uu-nnu-va-di

ROD - Rod of Moses was the one he used to part the Red sea (Exodus 14:16)

ഊ ഊ

ഊ ഊ

ഋ

Eru
ഋതു
Eru-tu

SEASON- Jesus calmed the storm.
(Mathew 8:23-27)

ഋ ഋ

ഋ ഋ

എ

Ae
എസ്തർ
Esther

Esther- who was promoted to a Queen in the Bible saved all the jewish people in her kingdom from being killed.

എ എ

എ എ

ഏ Aae

ഏദൻതോട്ടം

Aae-dan Tho-ttam

The GARDEN OF EDEN is in the first book of the Bible- Genesis. Read Genesis 2:15

ഐ

ഐ

EYE- Jesus touched the EYE and healed the BLIND.
Mark 8: 22-25

ഐ ഐ

ഐ ഐ

O

ഒബദ്യാവ്

O-bdha-vau

OBADIAH- The book of Obadiah is the shortest book of the Old Testament.

ഒ   ഒ

ഒ   ഒ

ഓ

Oo

ഓടി
Oo-di

RUN- In Mark 16:1-8, Mary Magdalene ran to the tomb of Jesus after sunrise and found that the tomb stone has been rolled away.

ഓ ഓ
_____

ഓ ഓ
_____

ഔ

Ou

ഔഷധം

Ou- sha- dham

MEDICINE- In Luke 5:31, Jesus is referred to as the Great Physician

ഔ ഔ

ഔ ഔ

അം

Aam

അംഗം

Aam-gam

MEMBER-The members of the Church are called ANGAMs' of the Church.

അം അം

അം അം

അം Aaa

CONSONANTS 15

ക

Ka
കൃസ്തു

Kri- sthu

JESUS- is the epicentre of Christanity.
Colossians: 1:18

ക   ക

ക   ക

ഖ

Kha
മു**ഖ**ം

Mu- kha-m

FACE- We all look to the FACE of Jesus with hope.
2 Corinthians- 3: 18

ഖ   ഖ

ഖ   ഖ

ഗ

Ga

ഗൊൽഗോഥാ

Gol-go-tha

GOLGOTHA- means 'Place of the skull'. It is the place where Jesus was crucified.

ഘ

Gha

മേഘം

Me-gha-m

CLOUD- He covers the heavens with clouds, he prepares rain for the earth. Psalm: 147: 8

ഘ ഘ
_____

ഘ ഘ
_____

ങ

Nga

തേങ്ങി

The-ngi

WEPT- Women of Jerusalem wept when they saw Jesus on the cross. (Luke 23: 27-31)

ങ ങ

ങ ങ

20

لد

Cha

لدَ

Cha-tta

WHIP- Jesus used a WHIP and cleared the merchants out of the Temple of Jerusalem.
John 2:15

Chha

ഛായ

Chha-ya

RESEMBLANCE- When Jesus appears we shall be like him.
1 John 3:2

ഛ ഛ

ഛ ഛ

Ja

ജ**ലം**

Ja- lam

WATER- John the Baptist baptised Jesus in the Jordan River. (Luke 3: 21-22)

ജ   ജ
_____

ജ   ജ
_____

Tha

തയഷം

Tha- sham

FISH- Jesus feeds 5000 people with 2 FISH.
Mathew:14: 13-21

തയ   തയ
_____

തയ   തയ
_____

ഞ

Nja
ഞായർ

Nja-yar

SUNDAY - The day you go to your Church.

ഞ   ഞ
_____

ഞ   ഞ
_____

S

Tah
പS

Pa-tah

ARMY- The walls of Jerico crumbled when Joshua and his ARMY marched around the city. Joshua 6: 20

S   S

S   S

Dha

പാഠം

Pa-dha-m

LESSON- Give instructions to a wise man, and he will be yet wiser: Proverbs. 9: 9

O O

O O

ഡ

Da
ഡാനിയേൽ
Da-niel

DANIEL- Daniel was thrown into a den of lions, but God saved him. (Daniel : 6: 16-23)

ഡ   ഡ

ഡ   ഡ

വഴ

Edha
മൂവഴൻ
Moo-dha-n

FOOL- The FOOL says in his heart ' There is no God'.
Psalm 14: 1

വഴ വഴ

വഴ വഴ

Nah

പണം

Pa-nam

MONEY- Jesus was betrayed by Judas for 30 pieces of silver. Mathew 26: 16

ണ   ണ
_____

ണ   ണ
_____

ത

Ta
തല

Ta-la

HEAD- Christ is the HEAD of the Church & Church is his body.(Colossians: 1:18)

ത   ത

ത   ത

Etha
കഥ

Ka-etha

STORY- New Testment is the STORY of Christ.

ß

Da
ßഡ

Da-ya

KINDNESS- Jesus showed KINDNES to the sick, and healed them with his touch.
Mathew: 8: 1-4

ß ß

ß ß

ധ

Dha
ബാധ

Ba- dha

PLAGUE- God brought about PLAGUES in Egypt at the time of Moses. (Exodus 9: 14-16)

ധ   ധ
_____

ധ   ധ
_____

Na
നാക്ക്

Na-kku

TONGUE- The TONGUE is a small part of the body, but it makes great boasts.
James 3: 5-6

പ

Pa
പ്രാർത്ഥന
Pra-artha-na

PRAYER
PRAYER brings victory.
Psalms : 108: 13

പ   പ

പ   പ

Pha
ഫലം
Pha-lam

FRUIT- What are the FRUITS of the Spirit ?
Read Galatians: 5: 22-23

ബ

Ba
ബൈബിൾ
Bible

BIBLE- Your word is a lamp for my feet, a light on my path.
Psalm 119: 105

ബ ബ

ബ ബ

Bhha
ഭക്തി
Bhha-kti

FAITH
FAITH can move mountains.
Mathew 17:20

Ma
മശിഹാ
Ma-si-ha

MESSIAH
Jesus is referred as MESSIAH - The Saviour King.
Mathew 1:16

ယ

Ya

ယေရှု
Ye-shu

JESUS
Jesus Christ is the Saviour and our Lord.
Titus 2:13

ര

Ra
രക്ഷകൻ
Ra-ksha-kan

SAVIOUR
Let's accept Jesus as our Saviour.
Romans: 10:9

ര ര

ര ര

ല

La
മ**ല**

Ma-la

MOUNT
Mount of Calvary was were Jesus was crucified.
Luke 23: 33

Va

വേദപുസ്തകം
Va-da-pusta-kam

BIBLE
BIBLE is the word of God.
It is the lamp for our feet.
Psalm : 119: 105

ശ

Sha
മോശ
Mo-sha

MOSES
Moses leads Israelites out of Egypt and through the Red sea. (Exodus 14)

ശ ശ

ശ ശ

Szha

സാക്ഷ്യം

Sha-ksh-yam

TESTIMONY
Your life is your biggest TESTIMONY of your faith.
Mathew: 5: 16

സ

Sa

സണ്ടേ സ്കൂൾ

Sunday school

SUNDAY SCHOOL- Train up a child in the way he should go; even when he is old he will not depart from it. Proverbs 22: 6

സ സ

സ സ

Ha

ഹല്ലേലുയ്യ

Halle-lu-jah

HALLELUJAH in Hebrew means 'Praise the Lord'

ഹ ഹ

ഹ ഹ

ള

Laa
തവള

Tha-va-laa

FROG- During the time of Moses, God sends a plague of FROGS to Egypt. (Exodus : 8)

ള ള

ള ള

Yza

ഩയ

Ma-yza

RAIN- The Lord will open to you his good treasure in the sky, to give the rain of your land in its season Deuteronomy 28: 12

Ra

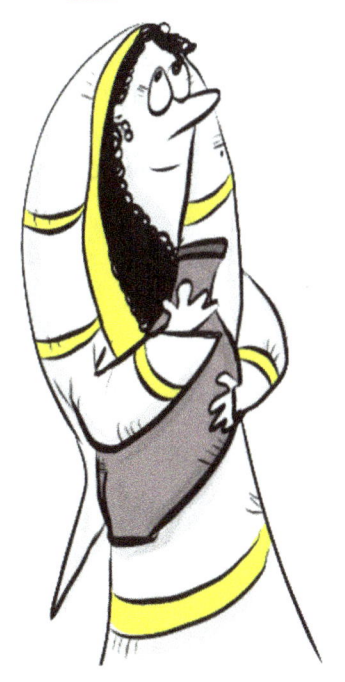

റബേക്ക

Ra-be-cca

REBECCA- In the book of Genesis in the Bible, REBECCA is the wife of Issac. (Genesis : 24)

TO MY WONDERFUL NEVA & AIDEN

First published by LIGHT AUSTRALIA in 2026

Text and Illustrations copyright (c) Dr. Abraham Thomas , 2026.

Dr. Abraham Thomas asserts his moral rights as the author and illustrator of this book.

Design and Layout by Dr. Abraham Thomas

All rights reserved. Without limiting the rights under copyright reserved above, no part of this publication may be reproduced, stored in or introduced into a database and retrieval system or transmitted in any form or any means (electronic, mechanical, photocopying, recording or otherwise) without the prior written permission of the author, unless specifically permitted under the Australian Copyright Act 1968 as amended.

The digital illustrations of this book is created by Dr. Abraham Thomas

Type set in Myriad Pro

Printed in Australia

ISBN: 978-0-6457217-5-1

A catalogue record of this book is available from the National Library of Australia

www.ingramcontent.com/pod-product-compliance
Lightning Source LLC
Chambersburg PA
CBHW051215290426
44109CB00021B/2463